C000140480

How My Light Is Spent

Alan Harris

Royal Exchange Theatre, Manchester
24 April – 13 May 2017

Sherman Theatre, Cardiff
16 – 27 May 2017

Theatre by the Lake, Keswick
31 May – 24 June 2017

The first performance of *How My Light Is Spent* was
at the Royal Exchange Theatre on 24 April 2017

How My Light Is Spent

by Alan Harris

CAST

JIMMY	Rhodri Meilir
KITTY	Alexandria Riley

CREATIVE TEAM

DIRECTOR	Liz Stevenson
DESIGNER	Fly Davis
LIGHTING DESIGNER	Joshua Pharo
SOUND DESIGNER	Giles Thomas
MOVEMENT	Polly Bennett
ASSISTANT DIRECTOR	Andy Routledge
CASTING DIRECTOR	Jerry Knight-Smith CDG
STAGE MANAGER	Sarah Goodyear
STAGE MANAGEMENT INTERN	Annie Fletcher
PRODUCTION MANAGER	Greg Skipworth

THE COMPANY

RHODRI MEILIR (Jimmy) studied drama at Aberystwyth University and was awarded a Fellowship of the University in 2014. Theatre credits include: *The Funfair* (HOME Manchester); *Bright Phoenix* (Liverpool Everyman); *Mametz* (National Theatre Wales) and several productions for Theatr Genedlaethol Cymru, Theatr Bara Caws and Cwmni'r Frân Wen. Television credits include: *Afterlife, My Family, Doctor Who* and *The Hogfather*. Rhodri has appeared in several different series for the channel S4C, including: *Anita, Y Gwyll/Hinterland, Byw Celwydd, Y Pris, Pen Talar, Caerdydd, Rapsgaliwn, Teulu* and *Tipyn O Stâd*. In 2013 he was nominated as best actor by Bafta Cymru for his role as Trefor in *Gwlad Yr Astra Gwyn*. Film credits include: *Pride, Under Milk Wood/Dan Y Wenallt, Y Syrcas, Mr Torquay's Holiday, Patagonia* and *Ble Mae Cyw?*. Rhodri can be heard in many Radio 4 and Radio Cymru plays and is also the voice of Michelangelo in S4c's Welsh-language version of *Teenage Mutant Ninja Turtles*.

ALEXANDRIA RILEY (Kitty) graduated from Royal Welsh College of Music and Drama. Previous credits include: *The Mountaintop,* for which she received a best actress nomination in the Wales Theatre Awards (The Other Room); *All That I Am* (Sherman Theatre/Royal Welsh College of Music and Drama/Gate). Radio credits include: *The Wide Sargasso Sea, Britt-Marie Was Here*.

ALAN HARRIS (Writer) plays include: *Love, Lies and Taxidermy* (Paines Plough/Sherman Theatre/Theatr Clwyd); *The Opportunity of Efficiency* (New National Theatre Tokyo/National Theatre Wales); *The Magic Toyshop* (Invisible Ink/Theatr Iolo); *The Future for Beginners* (liveartshow/ Wales Millennium Centre); *A Good Night Out in the Valleys* (National Theatre Wales); *A Scythe of Time* (New York Musical Theatre Festival); *Cardboard Dad* (Sherman); *Orange* (Sgript Cymru). He has also written for BBC Radio 4 and Radio 3. Libretti include: *Marsha: A Girl Who Does Bad Things* (liveartshow/Arcola Grimeborn Festival); *The Hidden Valley* (Birdsong Opera/Welsh National Opera/Tête à Tête); *The Journey* (Welsh National Opera); *Rhinegold, Manga Sister* (both liveartshow/The Yard, London). He won a Judges'Award at the 2015 Bruntwood Prize for *How My Light Is Spent*.

LIZ STEVENSON (Director) is the Associate Director at Theatre by the Lake where she will be directing *Handbagged* and *The Secret Garden*. Liz won the JMK Young Director Award in 2015, for which she was awarded the opportunity to direct her production of *Barbarians* at the Young Vic. The production was nominated for an Olivier Award for Outstanding Achievement in an Affiliate Theatre. In 2015 her production of *We Are The Multitude* for 24:7 Theatre Festival was nominated for a Manchester Theatre Award. After studying English at the University of Nottingham, she trained on the Theatre Directing MFA at Birkbeck, University of London. She has been an assistant director for the Royal Exchange, Hampstead Theatre, Shakespeare's Globe, Menier Chocolate Factory and The Gate. She is the Artistic Director of Junction 8 Theatre.

FLY DAVIS (Designer) has previously designed *A Streetcar Named Desire*, *Scuttlers*, *Hunger for Trade* and *Nothing* for the Royal Exchange Theatre. Other design credits include: *Othello* (Shakespeare's Globe); *Barbarians* (Olivier nominated; Young Vic); *The Winter's Tale* (Lyceum); *Trade* (Young Vic); *The Remains of Masie Duggan* (Abbey, Dublin); *A Million Tiny Plays About Britain* (Watermill), *Unreachable* (costume design, Royal Court); *Contractions* (Sheffield Crucible); *The Comedy of Errors, I Want My Hat Back* (National Theatre; Olivier nominated); *The Glass Menagerie* (Headlong/West Yorkshire Playhouse/Liverpool Playhouse/Richmond); *Unreachable* (costume design, Royal Court); *Opera For The Unknown Woman* (Fuel UK tour); *The Crocodile* (Manchester International Festival/Invisible Dot); *James and the Giant Peach* (West Yorkshire Playhouse); *I'd Rather Goya Robbed Me of My Sleep Than Some Other Arsehole, Image of an Unknown Young Woman* (Gate); *Turning a Little Further, A Streetcar Named Desire* (Young Vic); *Primetime, Pigeons, Collaboration* (Royal Court); *Eye of a Needle, Superior Donuts* (Southwark Playhouse); *The Dissidents* (Tricycle); Russell Kane's *The Great British Country Fete Musical* (Bush/UK tour); Nick Mohammed's *Dracula! (Mr Swallow the Musical)* (Soho Invisible Dot); *A Million Tiny Plays About Britain* (Watermill); *Woyzeck* (Omnibus); *What the Animals Say* (Greyscale UK tour). *The Invisible Dot's Big Birthday Bash* (Hammersmith Apollo); *Love is Easy* (McFly music video). Awards: Off West End Award Best Set Design, Best Production for *Image of an Unknown Young Woman* (Gate).

JOSHUA PHARO (Lighting Designer) recent credits include: *The Twits* (Curve, Leicester); *Removal Men* (The Yard); *Burning Doors* (Belarus Free Theatre); *Broken Biscuits* (Paines Plough); *The Future* (Company Three); *Contractions* (Sheffield Crucible); *Julie* (Northern Stage); *We're Stuck!* (China Plate); *Giving* (Hampstead); *Iphigenia Quartet, In The Night Time* (*Before The Sun Rises*), *Medea* (Gate); *The Rolling Stone* (Orange Tree); *Glass Menagerie* (Nuffield, as Video Designer); *The Merchant of Venice, Wuthering Heights, Consensual* (Ambassadors); *The Crocodile* (Manchester International Festival); *One Arm* (Southwark Playhouse); *The Trial Parallel, A Streetcar Named Desire Parallel* (Young Vic); *Amadis De Gaulle* (Bloomsbury); *Beckett Season* (Old Red Lion); *The Deluge* (UK tour, Lila Dance); *Usagi Yojimbo* (Southwark Playhouse); *Pioneer* (UK tour, Curious Directive); *I'd Rather Goya Robbed Me of My Sleep, No Place Like Home* (The Gate); *Thumbelina* (UK tour, Dancing Brick).

GILES THOMAS (Sound Designer) composition and sound design credits include: *Wish List, Yen* (Royal Exchange/Royal Court); *Pomona* (Royal Exchange); *Death of a Salesman* (Royal & Derngate); *Othello* (Tobacco Factory, Bristol); *Contractions* (Sheffield Theatres); *Correspondence* (Old Red Lion); *I See You, Wolf from the Door, Prime Time, Mint, Pigeons, Death Tax, The President Has Come To See You* (Royal Court); *Pomona* (National Theatre/Royal Exchange/ Orange Tree; Offie Nomination, Best Sound Designer); *Sparks* (Old Red Lion); *The Titanic Orchestra, This Will End Badly, Allie* (Edinburgh); *Little Malcolm and His Struggle Against the Eunuchs* (Southwark Playhouse); *Outside Mullingar* (Theatre Royal Bath); *Back Down* (Birmingham Rep); *Lie With Me* (Talawa); *The Sound of Yellow* (Young Vic); *Take a Deep Breath and Breathe, The Street* (Ovalhouse). Sound designs include: A Dark Night In Dalston (Park); *What Shadows* (Birmingham Rep); *They Drink It In The Congo* (Almeida); *The Sugar-Coated Bullets of the Bourgeoisie* (Arcola/HighTide Festival); *Orson's Shadow, Superior Donuts* (Southwark Playhouse); *Betrayal* (UK tour); *The Snow Queen* (Nuffield/Royal & Derngate); *A Harlem Dream* (Young Vic); *Khandan* (Birmingham Rep & Royal Court); *Three Men in a Boat* (UK tour); *King John* (Union); *It's About Time* (nabakov); *Shoot/Get Treasure/Repeat* (Out of Joint).

POLLY BENNETT (Movement Director) theatre includes: *Don Juan in Soho* (Wyndham's); *Junkyard* (Headlong); *My Country: A Work in Progress* (National Theatre); *Travesties* (Menier Chocolate Factory/West End); *A Streetcar Named Desire* (Royal Exchange Theatre); *Blush* (Underbelly); *The Deep Blue Sea* (National Theatre); *Doctor Faustus* (Duke of York's); *People, Places & Things* (National Theatre/West End); *The Maids* (Trafalgar Studios); *A Midsummer Night's Dream* (RSC); *Yen* (Royal Court/Royal Exchange); *The Lion, the Witch and the Wardrobe* (Birmingham Rep); *Plaques and Tangles* (Royal Court); *The Whipping Man* (Plymouth Theatre Royal); *Pomona* (National Theatre/Royal Exchange/Orange Tree); *Three Days in the Country* (National Theatre); *Songs for a New World* (St. James Theatre); *hang* (Royal Court); *The Famous Victories of Henry V* (RSC/tour); *The Rise and Fall of Little Voice* (Birmingham Rep/West Yorkshire Playhouse); *The Angry Brigade* (Bush); *A Mad World My Masters* (RSC); *Dunsinane* (National Theatre Scotland); *The King's Speech* (Chichester/Birmingham Rep); *To Kill a Mockingbird* (Regent's Park). Other work includes *Gareth Malone's Best of British* for the BBC; Fazer's Urban Symphony for the Royal Albert Hall/BBC; Assistant Movement Director on the London 2012 Olympics Opening Ceremony, Mass Cast Choreographer on the London 2012 Paralympic Opening Ceremony and Mass Cast Choreographer on Sochi Winter Olympics Opening Ceremony.

ANDY ROUTLEDGE (Assistant Director) is resident Assistant Director for Royal Exchange as part of his Theatre Directing MFA at Birkbeck University. He studied English with Creative Writing at University of Nottingham. Andy's directing credits include: *Year Ten* (Tabard); *Carnival* (Nottingham Lakeside Arts); *The 39 Steps, East, Krapp's Last Tape* (Nottingham New Theatre). Assisting credits include: *Twelfth Night, You, The Audience Manifesto, Sweet Charity, A Streetcar Named Desire, B!Rth* (Royal Exchange Theatre); *Port* (Arts Ed); *A Christmas Carol* (Old Red Lion). Andy co-devised *Ventoux With 2magpie*s (national tour) and played elliot in *Mercury Fur* (Stephen Joseph) as part of NSDF 13.

Manchester's Royal Exchange Theatre Company transforms the way people see theatre, each other and the world around them.

Our historic building, once the world's biggest cotton exchange, was taken over by artists in 1976. Today, our historic building is an award-winning cultural charity that produces new theatre in-the-round, in communities, on the road and online.

Exchange remains at the heart of everything we make and do. Now our currency is brand new drama and reinvigorated classics, the boldest artists and a company of highly skilled makers – all brought together to trade ideas and experiences with the people of Greater Manchester (and beyond).

The Exchange's unique auditorium is powerfully democratic, a space where audiences and performers meet as equals, entering and exiting through the same doors. It is the inspiration for all we do; inviting everyone to understand the past, engage in today's big questions, collectively imagine a better future and lose themselves in the moment of a great night out.

Our Spring Summer Season continues with the world premiere of Jane Austen's *Persuasion*, adapted and directed by Jeff James, and *Fatherland* – a world premiere co-created by Scott Graham, Karl Hyde and Simon Stephens as part of Manchester International Festival.

Find out more at **royalexchange.co.uk**

 instagram.com/rxtheatre

 facebook/rxtheatre

youtube.com/royalexchange.co.uk

Box Office **0161 833 0933**

 **AGMA** ASSOCIATION OF GREATER MANCHESTER AUTHORITIES

 MANCHESTER CITY COUNCIL

 Supported using public funding by **ARTS COUNCIL ENGLAND** LOTTERY FUNDED

Registered Charity Number 255424

ROYAL EXCHANGE THEATRE STAFF

CATERING
Catering General Manager
Ellen O'Donnell
Bars Manager
Chris Wilson
Hospitality Manager
Claire Molineux Jones
Supervisor
Mark Beattie
Supervisor
Jake Tysome
Head Chef
Chris Watson Gunby
Catering Team
Chris Gray, Paul
Roberts, Damien
Traczyk, Claudia
Codreanu, Alessia
Galli, Scott Pinion,
Daniele Codreanu
Front of House Team
Sarah Hope, Paul
Callaghan, Holly
Williams, Helen
Thomason, Jose Garcia
Carrasco, Simon
Mayne, Cat Belcher,
Emma Gold, Leah
Curran, Robin Lyons,
Vicky Bowen, Adam
Abreu, Anouchska
Czmil, Gemma
Harmer, Hazel Durling,
Jo Fountain, Joe Lester,
Mark Newsome, Nick
Edmead, Phil Hanley,
Tom Johnson
DEVELOPMENT
Development Director Val Young
Senior Development Manager
Gina Fletcher
Individual Giving Manager
Becky Rosenthal
Corporate Development Manager
Christina Georgiou
Development Executive Holli Leah
Membership Manager
Jessica Hilton
DIRECTORATE
Executive Director
Mark Dobson
Artistic Director
Sarah Frankcom
Associate Artistic Directors
Amit Sharma,
Matthew Xia

Associate Artists
Maxine Peake, Benji
Reid, Chris Thorpe
Assistant to the Artistic Directorate & Executive Director Michelle Hickman
Birbeck Trainee Director
Andy Routledge
ELDERS COMPANY
Liz Aniteye, Janice
Bonner, Tony Cocker,
Val Collier, Shelia
Colman, Christine
Connor, Phyllis Day,
Marianne Downes,
Gordon Emerson,
Monica Farry, Tommy
Flaherty, Graham Gillis,
Norman Goodman,
Philip Haynes, Brenda
Hickey, Amina Latimer,
Christopher Littler,
Jacquie Long, Estelle
Longmore, Charles
McDermott, Donald
McGregor, Alan
Maguire, Dudley
Newell, Sandy
Parkinson, Doreen
Robinson, Pauline
Sergeant, Maureen
Stirpe, Anne Tober,
Glyn Treharne, Anne
Walton, David Weston,
Michael Williams, Jean
Wood, Judith Wood
ENGAGEMENT
Director of Engagement
Amanda Dalton
Head of Participation and Learning Sarah Lovell
Participation and Learning Producer
Chris Wright
Adults Programme Leader Andy Barry
Young People's Programme Leader
Matt Hassall
Schools Programme Leader
Chelsea Morgan
Youth Engagement Programme Leader (Outreach)
Parvez Qadir
Community Programme Leader
Tracie Daly
Administrator
Emma Wallace
Admin Assistant
Allan Foy

FINANCE & ADMINISTRATION
Director of Finance & Administration
Barry James
HR Manager
Yvonne Cox
Administrator
Melissa Brakel
Finance Manager
Sue Jones
Orders & Purchase Ledger Clerk
Jennifer Ellis
Payroll Clerk
Carl Robson
Finance Administrator
Elizabeth Coupe
GREEN ROOM
Supervisor
Yvonne Stott
Assistant Anne Dardis
MARKETING
Director of Marketing & Communications
Claire Will
Head of Marketing
Vanessa Walters
Communications Manager
Paula Rabbitt
Marketing Officer – Groups, Education & Development
Eleanor Higgins
Marketing Officer – Digital and Systems
Vicky Wormald
Marketing Officer
Anneka Morley
Digital Marketing Officer
Ashley McKay
Box Office Manager
Sue Partington
Box Office Assistants William
Barnett, Jon Brennan,
Lindsay Burke, Tracey
Fleet, Dan Glynn, Zoe
Nicholas, Christine
Simpson, Eleanor Walk
OPERATIONS
Operations Director
Jo Topping
Visitor Experience Manager
Lynne Burgon
Deputy Visitor Experience Manager
Stuart Galligan
Facilities Manager
David Mitchell

Hire & Events Assistant Linzi Hughes
Maintenance Technician
Carl Johnson
IT Manager
Ean Burgon
IT Support & Network Technician
John Barlow
Volunteer Coordinator
Kate Hardy
Shop Manager
Rachael Noone
Assistant Shop Manager Gail Owen
Shop Assistants
Elisa Robinson,
Clare Sidebotham,
Amber Samuels, Emily
Tilzey, Jessica Sharp
Duty Managers Jill
Bridgeman, Helen
Coyne, Rachel Davies
Head Ushers
Tracey Fleet, Heather
Madden, Stuart Shaw
Security Liam Ainsworth,
Liam Carty, Dave
Hughes, Anthony
Portman-Jones, Mike Seal
Stage Door
Thomas Flaherty,
Peter Mainka
Ushers Tom Banks,
Georgie Brown, Helen
Brown, Natasha Bybik,
Elizabeth Callan, Liam
Carty, Emily Chadwick,
Richard Challinor, Alicia
Cole, Elizabeth Coupe,
Chris Dance, Anna
Davenport, Cliona
Donohue, Luther
Edmead, Harry Egan,
Amy Claire Evans, Paul
Evans, Neil Fenton, Beth
Galligan, Wesley
Harding, Connie
Hartley, Jennifer Hulman,
Dan Lizar, Ben Lucas,
Heather Madden,
Sue McGonnell,
Tony O'Driscoll,
Elle Pemberton Steer,
Alice Proctor, John Roy,
Stuart Shaw, Vincent
Tuohy, Edward (Ted)
Walker, Judith Wood,
Mahdi Zadeh
Cleaning Contractors
Head Cleaner
Lillian Williams

Cleaners
Gillian Bradshaw,
Susan Burroughs,
Elaine Connolly,
Valarie Daffern,
Jackie Farnell, Ahab
Mohamed, Maryam
Murmin, Daniel
Thompson, Hussein
Fatima Yassin
PRODUCTION
Head of Production
Simon Curtis
Props Buyer Kim Ford
**Production
Coordinator**
Greg Skipworth
Driver John Fisher
Head of Technical
Richard Delight
Head of Sound
Sorcha Williams
**Senior Sound
Technicians**
David Norton,
Matt Simms
Sound Technician
Matthew Masson
Head of Lighting
Mark Distin-Webster
**Senior Lighting
Technicians**
Alex Dixon,
Matthew Lever
Lighting Technician
Louise Anderson
**Technical Stage
Manager**
Andy Roberts
Stage Technicians
Simon Wild,
Luke Murray
**Head of Props and
Settings** Neil Gidley
**Deputy Head of
Props and Settings**
Andy Bubble
**Workshop
Supervisor**
Carl Heston
Senior Scenic Artist
Phil Costello
Prop Makers
Ben Cook, Stuart
Mitchell, Meriel Pym,
Sarah Worrall
Head of Wardrobe
Nikki Meredith
**Deputy Head of
Wardrobe** Tracy Dunk
**Studio Wardrobe
Supervisor**
Felicia Jagne
**Tailor & Gents
Cutter**
Rose Calderbank
Cutters Jennifer Adgey,
Rachel Bailey

**Hair and Make-up
Supervisor**
Jo Shepstone
**Costume Hire
Manager**
Ludmila Krzak
With help from the
volunteer team
**PROGRAMME
Senior Producer**
Ric Watts
**Casting Director &
Associate Director**
Jerry Knight-Smith CDG
Company Manager
Lee Drinkwater
**New Writing
Associate**
Suzanne Bell
Producer Amy Clewes
**Literary & Talent
Development
Administrator**
Davinia Jokhi
**Bruntwood Prize
Coordinator**
Chloe Smith
Assistant Producer
Max Emmerson
**YOUNG COMPANY
Associates** Afraa
Farhat, Afshan Ali, Ben
Hardy, Ella Dearden,
Lewis Lloyd, Maya
Bryan, Miriam
Abdulameer, Monica
Borovska, Samira
Chirzai, Tia Berry,
William Johnston, Zahi
Wade, Zeeshan Saeed
Communicators
Babsie Keulemans,
Chloe Green, Eleanor
Herbert, Furera Nelson-
Riggott, Hannah Dutson,
Jack Graham, Michael
Dwan, Milly Haire,
Molly Wilkinson,
Rizwana Ali, Tiffany
Bowman
Creatives Anna
Berentzen, Tyler
Holland, Yandass
Ndlovu, Christopher
Brown, Leah Whyment,
Mica Sinclair, Justina
Aina, Natalie Davies,
Nina Barber
Performers
Adam Hussain, Anna
Marshall, Charles
Jackson Goyea, Daisy
Robinson, Emilia Fagan,
Emily Cox, Fizz Shahid,
Georgia Lea, Helen Lau,
Kenya Sterling, Kyle
Garforth, Kylo Robinson,
Loren Fletcher, Lucas

Parker, Martha
Kershaw, Matthew
Allen, Matthew Mantel,
Mimi Johnson, Nathan
Walton, Nathan Burt,
Oliver Turner, Robyn
Henshaw, Roni Altman,
Sophie Edwards, Aarian
Mehrabani, Annie
Rogers, Anshula
Mauree-Bain, Benjamin
Maguire, Brogen
Campbell, Courtney
Butterfield, Daniel
Healiss, Ellie Burns,
Grainne Flynn, Isah-Levi
Green Roach, Jake
Mainwaring, Joe Clegg,
Joseph Basic, Josh
Hawson, Kenan Vurgun,
Krysia Milejski, Lauren
Greer, Matt Wikinson,
Oscar Jones, Shantel
Madziva, Sonny Poon
Tip, Tom Lyons, Victoria
Hoyle, Zak Ford-
Williams, Zoe Ndlovu
Technicians
Abigayle Bartley,
Alexandra Gaudel,
Heather Cohen, Holly
Patra, Kate Webster,
Rose Wagner-Revitt,
Sam Porter-Frakes
Writers
Angela Channell,
Charlotte Maxwell,
Declan Foley, Elizabeth
Logan, Emma Smith, Joe
McKie, Kiedis Quigley,
Liam Barker, Olivia
Hennessy, Rachel Fallon,
Rebecca Zahabi, Robyn
Macrory-Beaumont
**BOARD OF
TRUSTEES**
Tania Black
(Chair) Ben Caldwell
Cllr A Cox
Tony Gordon
Sinead Greenaway
Cllr Anne-Marie
Humphreys
Jean Oglesby
Sally Penni
Jennifer Raffle
Caroline Roberts-Cherry
Bernard Sharp
Geoffrey Shindler OBE
Martyn Torevell
Dave Roscoe
Aziz Rashid

DONORS, SUPPORTERS AND BENEFACTORS

PRINCIPAL FUNDERS

MAJOR SPONSORS

CHEETHAM BELL

PROJECT SUPPORTERS
After Digital
The Andrew Lloyd Webber
    Foundation
Beaverbrooks Charitable
    Trust
The Booth Charities
Arnold & Brenda
    Bradshaw
The Co-operative
    Foundation
Computeam
Duchy of Lancaster
    Benevolent Fund
Emerald Waterways
Esmée Fairbairn
    Foundation
The Eventhall Charitable
    Trust
Galloways Printers
Garfield Weston
    Foundation
The Granada Foundation
Susan Hodgkiss CBE
Jack Livingstone Charitable
    Trust
The J Paul Getty Jnr
    Charitable Trust
The John Thaw Foundation
The John Thomas Kennedy
    Charitable Foundation
King Street Townhouse
    Hotel
The Leche Trust
M.A.C Cosmetics
The Madeline Mabey Trust

Manchester Guardian
    Society
The Noël Coward
    Foundation
The Oglesby Charitable
    Trust
Ordinary People,
    Interesting Lives
The Paul Hamlyn
    Foundation
The Peter Henriques
    Foundation
Pinsent Masons Foundation
The PWC Foundation
The Raffle Family
The Rayne Foundation
Martyn & Valerie Torevell
Trinistar & M J Mapp

PRINCIPAL MEMBERSHIP
Bruntwood
Cheetham Bell
Edmundson Electrical
Havas Lynx
Regatta

ENCORE MEMBERSHIP
Acies Group
Beaverbrooks
Dewhurst Torevell

ASSOCIATE MEMBERSHIP
Addleshaw Goddard
Grant Thornton
HFL Building Solutions
Hollins Strategic Land
homes4u Group
King Street Townhouse
    Hotel
Levitt Bernstein
Mills & Reeve
Pinsent Masons
RSM
Sanderson Weatherall
Sapphire Systems
Smart Alex
Whitebirk Finance Ltd
5plus Architects

PATRONS £1000+ PA
Arnold & Brenda
    Bradshaw
Martin & Sarah Burrill
Ben & Maggie Caldwell
Maureen Casket
Meg Cooper
Barbara Crossley
Brendan & Ellen Flood
The Harrison Family
Nick & Lesley Hopkinson
Richard & Elaine Johnson
William & Ariel Lees-Jones
Sandy Lindsay MBE
Stuart Montgomery
Christine Ovens
Stephen & Judy Poster
& all our anonymous
    patrons

For more information on
how you can support the
work of the Royal
Exchange Theatre please
contact the Development
Department on
0161 615 6759

"It is easy to lose faith in an over subscribed industry that has very little funding to support new work, but the Bruntwood Prize is that opportunity. It changed my life."

Gareth Farr
Judges Prize winner of The Bruntwood Prize for Playwriting 2011
for his play *Britannia Waves The Rules*

The 2017 Bruntwood Prize for Playwriting submissions close on 5th June.

Over our 40-year history as one of Manchester's largest property companies, Bruntwood has always played an active part in the city and its community.

We are family owned and run, and have a strong belief that what is good for the cities we operate in is good for our customers and good for our business. That's why we are committed to pledging 10% of our annual profits to supporting the arts and other charitable and environmental activities.

THEATRE
by the
LAKE

'The most beautifully located and friendly theatre in Britain'
Independent

From our unique rural location, Theatre by the Lake produces excellent, ambitious and inspiring theatre for our audiences and participants, making nine shows a year as well as hosting a variety of festivals and visiting companies across our two theatre spaces.

2017 at Theatre by the Lake includes:

After the Dance
by Terence
Rattigan

Handbagged
by Moira Buffini

As You Like It
by William
Shakespeare

Miss Julie
by August
Strindberg in a new
adaptation by
Howard Brenton

Remarkable Invisible
by Laura Eason

The Secret Garden
by Frances
Hodgson Burnett
Adapted by
Jessica Swale

Box Office: 017687 74411
www.theatrebythelake.com

 @tbtlake

ARTS COUNCIL
ENGLAND
Supported using public funding by

Cumbria
County Council

Keswick Town Council

COMPELLING THEATRE FOR CARDIFF AND BEYOND

Based in the heart of Cardiff, Sherman Theatre is a leading producing house with a particular remit for the development and presentation of new writing.

We make and curate theatre for audiences in Wales, across the UK and internationally and develop the work of Welsh and Wales based artists. We generate opportunities for the citizens of Cardiff to connect with theatre through relevant, inspiring and visionary engagement.

Sherman Theatre is the first Welsh producing house to transfer work to the National Theatre; to perform at the Schaubühne, Berlin and to co-produce with the Royal Court Theatre, London. We make work with local relevance and international impact.

❛❛ SHERMAN THEATRE, WITH RACHEL O'RIORDAN AT THE HELM, IS A FORCE TO BE RECKONED WITH.❜❜

Exeunt, *A Doll's House*

✉ 029 2064 6900
shermantheatre.co.uk

f 🐦 📷 @ShermanTheatre

 Cyngor Celfyddydau Cymru
Arts Council of Wales

 Noddir gan
Lywodraeth Cymru
Sponsored by
Welsh Government

 Supported by
The National Lottery®
through the Arts Council of Wales

Cefnogwyd gan
Y Loteri Genedlaethol
trwy Gyngor Celfyddydau Cymru

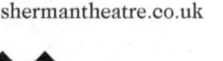 phf **Paul Hamlyn** Foundation

SHERMAN THEATRE STAFF LIST

Artistic Director Rachel O'Riordan

Executive Director Julia Barry

Head of Finance and Administration Sally Shepherd

Head of Production and Planning Nick Allsop

Head of Marketing and Communications Ed Newsome

Administrator Lauren Aldridge

Artistic Coordinator Sarah Jones

Associate Director Gethin Evans

Box Office Manager Liz Thomas

Company Stage Manager Chris Peterson

Deputy House Manager Keira Wilkie

Café Bar Supervisor Robin Hannagan-Jones

Finance Assistant Julia Griffiths

Fundraising Manager Emma Tropman

House Manager Andrew Lovell

Marketing Officer Rebecca Price

Scenic Carpenter Mathew Thomas

Senior Electrician Rachel Mortimer

Sherman 5 Marketing & Admin Assistant Siân Mile

Sherman 5 Coordinator Guy O'Donnell

Technical Stage Manager Stephen Blendell

Ticketing and Reception Assistants Beshlie Thorp, Elena Thomas, Ellen Thomas, Ethan Jenkins, Jack Law, Lizzie Ryder-Smith, Lynwen Haf Roberts, Scott Skelton, Tamar Williams

Wardrobe Manager Deryn Tudor

Youth and Community Associate Anna Poole

Creative Intern Nathan McCarthy

Thanks to our Café Bar team and our Front of House volunteers.

BOARD OF TRUSTEES

David Stacey (Chair)

Rosamund Shelley (Vice Chair)

Nicholas Carlton

Paul Clayton

Rhiannon Davis

Nick Gibbs

Marlies Hoecherl

Keith Morgan

Richard Newton

Sian Powell

Marc Simcox

Owen Thomas

HOW MY LIGHT IS SPENT

Alan Harris

Note on Play

This play was written for any number of performers, and the lines of dialogue can be divided up as future productions see fit. However, the original production was performed with two actors.

– at the end of a line indicates the next line following on immediately.

Italics are for real-time dialogue.

Narrative dialogue is not in italics.

This text went to press before the end of rehearsals and so may differ slightly from the play as performed.

Kitty, my hands have disappeared.

Pardon?

I woke up this morning and they were... In the night I could feel them seeping away. I woke up, held them up to the light shining through the blinds and there they weren't.

But how are you holding the, you know, phone?

I can still touch. But they aren't there. They've gone.

How do you feel?

Frightened.

And it's just your hands?

Do you think they'll come back?

Must admit, this is the first time, to be honest, you've thrown me a bit.

Not the reassuring answer I was hoping for.

You got to admit I'm not really qualified –

What'm I going to do?

Jimmy, no offence, but I'm a phone-sex worker –

But you're going to be a psychologist, you said.

Maybe put the phone down and try calling one-one-one?

When did Jimmy start to disappear?

This isn't just about Jimmy, there's Kitty –

And there's Mallary, altruism, robbery and losing your place in life and living with your mother, aspirations –

Turning invisible.

Fine. Okay. It started when Jimmy was at, uh, the start of it, I suppose, was at the drive-through doughnut –

No. Before that.

Getting the sack? Again.

Before that.

Ummm –

Masturbation.

Ahhh right. Fair enough, it goes back to that.

At precisely 7.30 p.m. on an unusually warm night in November, Jimmy picked up his Samsung Galaxy and –

Jimmy had considered having phone sex for a while.

In place of real sex?

Not really 'in place of' because the last time was, uh, a while ago.

He was, actually, quite nervous.

But quite erect.

A thirty-four-year-old man sitting in his mother's house in Newport –

Rita, his mother, was out –

She goes to the Salvation Army on Stow Hill; you know, the one next to the pet shop that has lizards in the –

She'd often try to get Jimmy to go with her –

God serves up a taste of hope for needy souls, Jimmy; there's free samples every Sunday.

Wednesday night was choir night at the Sally Army.

Jimmy was just glad to have the house to himself.

He set up the phone next to the bed.

Along with the business card he'd found in a phone box in Newport –

(One of the very few phone boxes in Newport town centre to still have a working phone in it.)

And a roll of toilet tissue.

Not exactly Andrex but soft enough and strong enough –

When Kitty answered the phone –

Good evening, this is Kitty –

He was already on the verge.

What should I call you?

Jimmy, the night before, had watched Troy on Film 4.

Umm, Hector.

From Kitty's point of view what followed was all very typical. Little did she know this was the start of a story for her too.

What you wearing?

Um, underwear. Bra, panties, you know?

What colour are they?

Red.

Has the thong got a lace trim?

Uh, yeah, it's very lacy.

You know I like those on you, right?

I knows it.

I need you to grab your titties.

Slow down, big –

Can you lick your own nipples?

I'll give it a go –

My hands are gliding across your skin. Tell me how they feel.

They feel good, they feels so, so good.

Yeah, that's what I'm talking about. Now, I need you to take your right hand and start playing with yourself. Can you do that for me, babe?

I'm doing it, I'm doing it.

You wet?

I got a lady boner.

Okay, I want you to –

Standard stuff.

Kitty was not wearing a thong.

She was, in fact, wearing sensible underwear.

The tracksuit she was wearing was not lacy.

She was definitely not 'wet'.

She did not have a lady boner.

While clients thought of her, Kitty thought of the cash.

She hated being called 'babe'.

Jimmy rang the sex line every Wednesday at 7.30 p.m.

The same line.

While his mother belted out 'Onward Christian Soldiers' on Stow Hill –

Speaking to the same woman. Kitty.

I know, not a particularly seductive name.

Kitty.

She felt it sounded vaguely exotic without being too threatening.

Kitty had built up a regular clientele:

Dennis was a Thursday as his wife had joined a netball team in an attempt to recapture her school days.

Maxi had access to a phone line working nights on security at Tredegar House.

(He would eventually be sacked after they got a two thousand and seventy-eight pound phone bill for the quarter.)

Jimmy was every Wednesday at 7.30 p.m.

It always started the same way.

What you wearing?

Masturbating.

What you doing now?

Masturbating.

What you –

You get the, uh, gist.

At one pound twenty pee a minute.

Minimum of nine minutes duration.

Jimmy never went over the nine minutes.

Not many clients do.

In fact, Jimmy was usually finished in about three minutes –

Leaving a little time to chat.

I'm successfully holding down a position in the booth at Newport's only drive-through doughnut restaurant –

I knows the one.

Restaurant is a bit of a fancy name for it to be honest –

Don't put yourself down, Hector.

Used to work at Panasonic for twelve years before they closed it down and moved the production line to Vietnam.

Right now there's probably someone who looks just like you –

A Vietnamese version –

Working in a factory in…

Binh Duong Province soldering pieces on to a DR765 board quicker than I ever could.

I'm sure you were very quick.

Uh, do you still live at home?

Let's talk about you, yeah? You're paying the bill.

I live with my mother. Seems like everyone still lives with the parents these days.

Jimmy told her about his ex-wife, Janet –

I was bad for her –

She was bad for him.

Ended very badly with her threatening to kill me with a kitchen knife after she'd caught me behind the Co-op with Keira Davey –

Allegedly a best friend of hers –

I actually said these very words: I think I can love two people.

Very naive.

Only good thing to come out of me and Janet was our daughter, Mallary –

She came out of Janet technically –

but I haven't seen her so much recently –

When was the last time you – ?

Four years –

You haven't seen your daughter in four years?

Uh, yeah, that's Janet for you, she cut off all access –

She'd wanted to cut his cock off but this was the next best thing.

To be fair, I think of Mallary every day –

To be fair?

Every time someone orders a 'birthday special' from Newport Nuts.

And that's – ?

*It consists of the amount of doughnuts for the person whose
birthday it is and some promotional crap. I once served seventy-
three doughnuts to a man whose mother was –*

I get it.

It caused a hell of a queue.

Jimmy had always thought: Are doughnuts really a good
birthday present?

Kitty shared no personal information with clients –

Not even regulars like Jimmy.

She kept her past – especially her childhood – locked up in a little
box that she never opened for anyone.

Jimmy would talk her through his working day:

At Newport Nuts you talk to a lot of people – if briefly.

And, after spending precisely nine minutes a week with Kitty –

Starting at exactly 7.30 p.m. –

For eight months –

Jimmy fell in love with Kitty.

Even though he knew very little about her.

She, too, had become curious about him. (Though she would
never admit it.)

Unlike Facebook where every time Kitty logged off she felt a
bit depressed, after Hector put the phone down she always felt a
bit brighter. Why was that?

At Newport Nuts Jimmy took the orders of the drive-through
customers via an intercom.

He liked to pretend he was an air traffic controller or a police
radio dispatcher:

*Roger that, two iced doughnuts and a Pepsi Max. That'll be
three ten. Proceed to the second booth for payment. Roger?*

Make it eight ten and that should pay for the car behind.

Really?

Kitty wondered if the man she was talking to was Hector…

That's… brilliant.

You think so?

That has made my day that has.

It's made my day to make someone's day. You're not going to just charge them anyway, are you?

I could, couldn't I!

You sound too… interesting for that.

Interesting sounding? Me? That really has made my day.

The car behind, naturally, had no idea that she was paying.

She didn't know them.

It was a German couple visiting Wales that had been heading for the bright lights of Cardiff but got the wrong turn-off and ended up in Newport.

It was a hell of a job telling them that they actually didn't have to pay.

Someone else has paid.

But we must pay now – it says so on your sign.

No, no, the woman in front, she has paid for you. She left a fiver and that's more than enough. You even get change.

But we don't know anyone here.

A week later.

That'll be three ten please. You have clearance to land at the next window.

Make it eight ten – a fiver for the car behind.

It's you. Again! Uh, do you fancy going out some time – for a bite to eat? With me. In person. Not here like, somewhere, uh, less doughnut-based?

They met for the first time –

In person –

At a dimly lit café in Commercial Street that sold everything for fifty pee – no matter what you had.

My name's Shelley.

No. It's not. Your name is Kitty. I recognise your voice. Or is your name really Shelley? Suppose it is – Kitty does sound a bit fake.

No, it really is Kitty.

It's you!

In the flesh.

She had gone into the phone-sex business and used her real name – Kitty – a mistake for a novice but –

Say something.

What?

Go on – say something.

Would you like to come on my tits – yes, you would, you dirty boy.

Fantastic!

Due to spending so much time talking hands-free Kitty had the inability to say anything quietly so the fifty-pee café was all ears after that.

Hector thinks you've been a bad girl, yes, you have! I'm not really called Hector, by the way, I'm called –

Am I like you imagined?

Definitely.

She didn't look like Jimmy had imagined –

Nor him to her –

But she was pleasant looking – nice eyes, a floral skirt.

Jimmy's tallness marked him out a bit – in a good way. He was no spring chicken but still had freckles and he had a sort of bowl-shaped haircut.

Jimmy's hair, in fact, was cut regularly by Rita using a bowl.

Her mixing bowl.

There followed a forty-three-second gap where Jimmy and Kitty took sips of tea and

Where you from, Kitty? You a Newport girl or –

Look –

West Wales? –

No, I –

Did you always want to be a phone-sex worker?

Please –

Yes?

I'd rather not talk about me.

Oh, right. Fair enough.

Another forty-three seconds:

So, why'd you do it?

The phone sex? Money.

Thought it would be.

I'm saving up to do a degree.

Bit late for that, isn't it?

What do you mean?

You've obviously been around the block a bit.

Jimmy wasn't very good at telling women what they wanted to hear.

Kitty ate her fifty-pee éclair.

Jimmy tried to recover:

It's mint that you, uh, you give some of your money away – at the drive-through.

Only a little.

Is that some kind of guilt thing? Cos you're a sex worker?

Just thought I'd see if I could be altruistic.

What?

He wasn't sure what altruism was so –

Had let her explain just enough before interrupting.

It's when people do something without any reward –

I know what it is, of course. Well, can you be, you know…? Can people be… altruism… istic?

Don't know yet.

What's your best guess?

It's tricky – I'm leaning towards the theory that every action we do is connected to sex.

Do you want another fifty-pee slice of cake?

Not for now.

Do you often, is this a regular thing you –

You're the first… client… I've ever met in person.

Lucky me.

Kitty then had an urge –

Not a sexual one like –

She felt the urge to say:

It's part of my research, the altruism. I'm going to retrain as a psychologist. What I've always wanted to be – a way to really help people.

Sounds pricey, anything that ends in 'ologist' sounds pricey.

What do you want, Jimmy?

I'd like to take up gardening.

Why don't you?

No garden.

Wise-ass.

Do you have a garden, Kitty?

I live in a house with a garden but it's not mine. My landlord likes topiary.

Jimmy had absolutely no idea what that was –

Maybe a form of nude gardening?

Kitty rented a granny flat in a nice house in Malpas that was owned by Stephen –

Who liked to be called Stevo –

Jessup.

Kitty had seen him this morning on her way out –

I'm thinking of cutting the hedge into a new shape, Kitty.

What shape?

I don't know. An animal?

Maybe a squirrel, Stevo?

Yes, maybe so.

Grey or red?

Sorry?

Squirrel. Grey or red?

Hmmm, I'm not so keen on the red squirrel.

Why's that, Stevo?

Flashy... buggers.

Sorry?

The red squirrel has a lot of support, granted. It's a much-loved mammal, only living in a few, select, pockets of Britain.

Yes, well –

Whereas the grey goes about its business quietly, the red... the red squirrel has blamed all its ills on the grey. We've taken it all as fact, haven't we? On face value. That the grey squirrel is to blame for the demise of the red squirrel. But do we know that? What has it actually done to it?

Jesus, she'd touched a nerve.

The red squirrel looks fantastic but could it have tried that little bit harder?

Back to the fifty-pee café –

In Commercial Street.

Wha's he like this, uh, Stevo character?

He's... solid.

Fat?

Of character.

Type of bloke your mother would like.

You don't know my mother.

Jimmy felt the meeting was getting away from him so he said:

Kitty, I –

Don't.

What?

Tell me you love me.

No, no, don't be silly, I wasn't going to say that. Do you think I'm mad!

We're too old for that game, Jimmy. We've both 'been around the block'.

Yeah, right. I'll never tell you I love you.

Promise?

Scouts' honour.

Fifteen people had told Kitty they loved her. It happened twice while growing up in Cardiff, twelve times on the phone-sex line –

In stages of pre –

During –

Or post –

Ejaculation.

And then there was the Stevo incident.

Exactly a year ago she'd come home late from watching the Toyota Masters snooker tournament at Newport leisure centre –

She considered snooker her secret vice –

Stevo had been waiting for her in the darkness – he'd been to a funeral reception for the chairman of the neighbourhood watch committee and drunk too much red wine –

Stevo was a tad over five feet tall –

Likes to wear tank tops, you know?

But today he was wearing a suit – and looked quite smart. Everything about him was proper – even the salt and pepper in his hair was immaculate.

You okay, Stevo? You crying?

Isn't it stupid, Kitty?

Didn't realise you and the chairman were so –

Is always there. We try not to think about death – until someone actually dies.

Stevo squared his shoulders, took both of Kitty's hands in his and said:

I think I love you.

Kitty had laughed it off as a joke and Stevo had never, ever, mentioned it since.

Of the fifteen people that told Kitty they loved her she had to admit Stevo had touched her the most – but she really didn't believe any of them.

Not one.

It was nice to meet you, Jimmy, thanks for the tea.

Will you still call at the drive-through to give money away? I honestly think it makes a difference to some people –

Of course I will.

The following day it happened.

Not sex with Kitty – she really couldn't be bought for tea and cake.

Jimmy was made redundant.

And, to be honest, we could have started the story here.

This is really where it starts, fair enough:

Jimmy, after another day in his booth, is pulled aside by his boss, Peake.

He'd once asked Peake what his first name was and Peake told him:

Haven't got one.

Ex-Army – you know the type –

One of those people who looks as though they're constantly busy but –

In fact –

Does fuck-all all day.

But he looks –

And sounds –

The business.

Probably does well in interviews.

His interview of Jimmy consisted of just one question:

Do you play squash, James?

This put Jimmy on the back foot.

Like tennis but indoors.

I know what squash is, Mr Peake.

Just Peake.

Smaller bats.

Racquets.

Time to lie:

Yes, I play squash.

They had never, ever played squash together while Jimmy worked there.

Jimmy had always wondered why Peake had asked about squash –

But dismissed it as Peake being Peake.

In fact, it was Peake's way of sifting out the weak; the people-pleasers.

He started by sacking the people who lied about playing squash.

When's it going to happen?

Today.

Like today today?

You're on a zero hours, yeah, the company don't have to give any notice.

Not even a –

Nothing, nada, zilch, zeroooooooooooooooooooo –

Peake was such a cock.

Couldn't you put me on a contract?

Sorry, the company is cutting –

Are you enjoying this?

I take no pleasure from this. The management is taking a leaf out of the Severn Crossing –

Which one?

Don't matter. People will now put their cash in a coin bin – when they've put in the requisite amount the barrier will open and they can drive away with their doughnut-based products.

But –

But nothing –

But –

But nothing –

I'm being replaced by a coin bin?

Jimmy was replaced by a coin bin.

Which has the advantage of lower costs and better traffic flow.

But it's impossible to pay for the car behind you.

When Jimmy said he 'had news', Rita hoped it was something positive.

Like Jimmy finally moving out and getting a place of his own.

She had designs of renting his room out on Airbnb.

Who the fuck's going to stay in Ringland?

Jimmy and Rita rarely spoke face to face.

He'd usually be in his bedroom and Rita would usually be in the kitchen.

She was on speed dial:

I've been sacked, Mum. Replaced. By a bin.

Rita's husband, Gregor, had left her when they lived in Llanelli.

No contact since for her or son Jimmy –

Not even a birthday card.

Several failed relationships, some good –

Some fucking terrible – including Jacob who stole all the savings she'd hidden in a bag of flour on Christmas Eve –

Resulting in her and Jimmy ending up in Ringland.

Newport.

Fucking Newport.

Even though she felt an outsider Rita did her damndest to fit in in Newport.

And wanted that for Jimmy too.

There might be jobs going at the new retail park, Friar's Walk –

That's when the tingling started in Jimmy's hands.

That's when the change happened.

When he realised –

What am I qualified to do after taking orders off doughnut eaters twenty times an hour?

You'll have to sign on.

Fuck.

Over in Malpas –

Kitty was paying Stevo his rent. In his living room.

In cash, as always.

Why dolls, Stevo?

People like porcelain, the way the light catches it. They order bespoke pieces online – and you can get a picture of your whole family on a giant tea mug.

The room was neat, like Stevo, but with an air of impermanence due to the number of boxes in it. Kitty knew Stevo sold stuff on eBay and was curious about the cabinet in the corner.

Why the display?

The cabinet was filled with porcelain figurines.

What are they –

That's the original collection. Mysian. Bagra. Turn-of-century. Schroeder. Pre-war. A Navarre.

You don't seem the type. To collect dolls.

He did.

Stevo opened up the cabinet.

My wife, Alexa, she started it and I just, it's funny what you can get in to, isn't it?

Trust me, Stevo, I've heard funnier.

Haven't opened this cabinet in six years. Saves dusting them.

They're beautiful.

They remind me of Alexa. Gave me the idea for the business.

Where is she, your wife?

She's happy. Has a son now.

He looked into Kitty's eyes.

Up and into Kitty's eyes.

Every time I look at the dolls it reminds me how easy it is to miss out on life. We always regret the things we don't do, not the things we do.

Kitty had to admit that Stevo did sometimes make sense.

She went upstairs and immediately called the man who had introduced her to the phone-sex industry.

Andre, I need to see you, that offer you made me, yes that one, I'd like to know more about it.

Kitty, my hands have disappeared.

Pardon?

I woke up this morning and they were… In the night I could feel them seeping away. I woke up, held them up to the light shining through the blinds and there they weren't.

But how are you holding the, you know, phone?

I can still touch. But they aren't there. They've gone.

How do you feel?

Frightened.

And it's just your hands?

Do you think they'll come back?

Must admit, this is the first time, to be honest, you've thrown me a bit.

Not the reassuring answer I was hoping for.

You got to admit I'm not really qualified –

What'm I going to do?

Jimmy, no offence, but I'm a phone-sex worker –

But you're going to be a psychologist, you said.

Maybe put the phone down and try calling one-one-one?

*Fuck that. Things are going from bad to worse, Kitty –
yesterday I lose my job and today I've lost my hands.*

Are you ever going to get up?

Don't feel well, Mum.

*Is it the job thing? Are you now going to develop some form of
depression?*

Please, can you just leave me –

Rita turned away from Jimmy's bedroom door – she was
more than happy to leave her son alone when he was in 'one
of his moods'.

For the rest of the day Jimmy stayed in bed.

Every now and again he'd pull his hands from out of the covers
to stare at where they used to be.

He tried to masturbate but it was so weird he couldn't get
a hard-on.

When he heard her go out, he got up, put on a pair of pants –

They said on the front:

Red meat only.

An inappropriate Christmas present from Rita.

And went downstairs for something to eat.

Eating a bowl of Cheerios was like an out-of-body experience.

The bowl, the milk, the box of cereal seemed to float in the air.

Fucking weird… And not in a good way.

Jimmy took no pleasure in this surreal sensation.

He retreated to bed –

Slid his arms under the covers and tried to sleep.

That proved impossible.

So, he picked up the phone and dialled.

Again.

I don't know what to do, Kitty.

Been thinking and I've decided it was a mistake – for us to ever meet.

I get this feeling, this hands thing, that this is just the start.

Jimmy?

What if the rest of me's going to disappear?

Look, I'm not being funny, but maybe this is just some kind of stress-related –

What have I got to be stressed about?

Maybe it's been building up?

The thing that is stressing me is losing my hands.

And your job and living with your mum and maybe, just maybe, it's related to your daughter.

How can this –

Maybe you're guilty about not seeing her?

Where the fuck has this come from?

We have things in life that lurk in the deep, they lie deep –

I am guilty, of course I feel guilty, but this –

Maybe you should see her.

Maybe you could stop saying maybe.

Just saying. Stress.

Time is running out –

No, you're nowhere near nine minutes –

I'm not on about the minimum spend! Can I see you?

No, as I said, I don't think that was –

Just for a bit. I'll show you my hands. You'll see.

See a doctor.

Before or after I see Mallary?

This is just a psychological –

It's not.

Okay.

You believe me?

But, maybe –

Stop saying maybe –

It's a symptom of something else. Of you being afraid of losing something?

For someone whose field this is not, you are full of fucking advice.

Think about it. And, Jimmy, you know how much I've enjoyed our… chats but from next Wednesday I won't be here.

Are you disappearing too?!

No, no, I'm taking a new line of work.

What do you –

Anyway –

Don't you dare say 'anyway' to me.

Look –

Tell me the truth.

I'm going to join an escort agency. If I work for them for six months I'll have enough money for the course I want to –

A prostitute?

Escort. A high-class –

Fuck. Exactly. This is about money, is it?

Isn't everything?

You can't just –

Sorry, Jimmy, our time's up.

Going on the game.

The phrase hit Kitty like a thunderbolt.

She had never considered –

Had kidded herself –

Andre said –

You'll most likely be accompanying men in tuxedos to gala events at the Celtic Manor.

Tuxedos signalled fair play and a gentleness and – shit – she'd created a fantasy where she'd be dating snooker players.

Her rising panic was interrupted by Stevo.

Kitty, you up there? I'm putting the kettle on.

Uh, yes, thank you, Stevo – I, yes, that's very kind of you.

Jimmy woke and checked his hands.

Still not there.

He heard Rita go out. Went to the bathroom.

Checked himself over in the mirror.

His left buttock had vanished.

Shit!

Later that day, on the phone to Rita, he casually mentioned he'd taken to wearing gloves.

You've got a what?

Skin condition.

What have you been touching? Have you been putting your hands down the toilet again?

Jimmy had, just once, retrieved a mobile phone from the bottom of the toilet without gloves and his mother had never gotten over it.

The conversation inevitably ended with Rita's latest mantra:

Have you signed on yet? I'm not keeping you.

Newport Jobcentre on Charles Street is a hellhole. Bouncers on the door. People hanging around and resenting it. Angry people.

Jimmy was being interviewed by a woman wearing too much make-up called Michelle.

His 'work coach' .

You can take off the gloves, sunshine.

I can't… skin condition. Is it okay to wear that much make-up in work?

When Michelle ignored this question –

Jimmy worried she really had some kind of terrible skin condition – now he'd embarrassed her.

In fact, Michelle couldn't give a flying fuck what anyone thought – not the bosses and certainly not the –

Clients.

She simply liked make-up.

Uh, I've had two jobs since leaving school – started at Panasonic (before we were all screwed over). For a while I felt like a cog in a well-oiled Japanese machine – we really did morning exercises. After Panasonic I moved on to Newport Nuts.

You saw this as career progression?

He'd dreamt that Peake would one day die of a heart attack –

Or something much more painful –

And he'd be hand-picked as manager.

He'd always thought himself as working class but now, what was he –

Non-class.

I suppose, Michelle, working here, at least it's safe?

You seen the security?

I mean the job is safe – you can't be replaced by a coin bin. Have you got any real jobs?

Sorry?

Making something?

I'll put you down for retail.

Nothing?

Retail.

Okay. Drive-through.

Not much call –

Drive-through.

Is that really realistic? You just been made redundant from Newport's only drive-through food outlet. You have to broaden your job-search criteria.

Can we try drive-through for a while?

You got to give yourself the best chance of gaining employment, sunshine, and, as your work coach, I'd say that is limiting your options.

Shouldn't have mentioned the make-up.

I'll put you down for retail. The new Friar's Walk development has –

No.

What?

Can't you just put down what I want?

You never filled out a Universal Job Match form, have you?

Jimmy could see that Michelle meant well.

But this wasn't going to work out.

Jimmy didn't get as far as –

Sign here, here, here, here and here.

He didn't get as far as the threat of sanctioning.

He was disappearing and, fuck it, if he sat in the dole any longer he felt that might speed his disappearance.

I'm thinking of seeing Mallary.

Why?

She's my –

Why now?

I've been trying to work some stuff out before –

Before what?

It's her birthday tomorrow.

You think she'll want to see you? You don't see someone for four years, then get in touch.

I need to do it now.

You'll need to take a present.

I know!

I'm coming upstairs, we need to talk about this properly.

Jimmy quickly put on a DVD and –

Lay in bed –

With his hat on.

Can I come in?

If you must.

You're watching something?

DVD.

That is a very sad film. Is there much to go?

What do you want?

I'm worried about you. Can we turn that off?

I'm watching it. When I watch something, Mum, as you know, I like to watch it in one go. If you pause and watch and pause and do something and pause and do something else you lose the thread.

About Mallary, love, can you –

What?

Tell her that I miss her and that I love her.

This is about as tender as Jimmy and Rita got.

She knew to leave now –

But Jimmy caught her before she closed the door.

Mum?

Love?

What happened with Dad? Did he disappear?

He did.

What happened?

He was here and then he was gone.

How long?

What?

How long did it take?

He was acting funny when he went to pick up his wages from the bakery on the Friday afternoon. The next week he went over there and I never saw him again.

A week?

Silly really, I said to him: 'It's spag bol for tea' but I knew he wouldn't be back.

Mum, it's not your fault. He disappeared.

You know what happens in the end, don't you?

What?

Your DVD.

Don't spoil the ending for me.

It doesn't end well, for him, the Invisible Man.

Thanks a bloody bunch.

Your dad and me.

Yes?

God gives each relationship a certain amount of light, Jimmy.

She might not wear the uniform but she was Salvation Army to the bone.

When that light is gone, then the love in that relationship dies. Bit like a candle. It can only burn for so long. Some lights can burn for a very long time – but for others, like me and your father –

Do you think it's true for people too?

What?

Are we like candles? Do we have a certain amount of light and when that's gone, we're gone?

I don't know, Jimmy. Are you okay, love?

With Rita safely back in the kitchen Jimmy picked up his phone:

Please don't go.

Sorry? Jimmy?

I want to keep on ringing you up and wank off when you pretend what you're doing. I don't want you to... go.

Please, Jimmy, I don't want this to be any more awkward –

Please.

What do you want from me, Jimmy?

I just said –

Time goes so quickly, Jimmy. It's easy to miss out on life.

Come on, Kitty, we're going to be late.

Yes, I'll be down in a minute.

Who's that?

That? Stevo.

We'd better make a move, Kitty.

Okay, Stevo, I'm just talking to a... friend.

I'll let you get on, Kitty.

As Jimmy pressed the red button on his phone, in black and white the Invisible Man unwrapped the bandages from around his head to reveal...

Maybe I shouldn't be watching this.

Jimmy watched Mallary.

She was shaking her phone.

Waiting.

Looking at the phone.

Shaking the phone again.

Waiting.

Repeat.

Mallary was startled to look up and see Jimmy standing on the edge of Coronation Park.

He was holding a large box and was –

Framed in the sunlight by the Transporter Bridge.

She wasn't like he remembered:

Wearing jeans and a Nirvana T-shirt, she now looked like a mini-Janet: from her fierce eyebrows to her quick movements.

He reminded her who he was straight away –

Men in parks is dangerous ground these days –

He rambled on for minutes about looking forward to seeing her for ages, he'd been bloody busy and he was wearing the gloves cos of a skin condition.

Is there anything you'd like to ask me, Mallary?

Why you wearing earmuffs?

Jimmy's ears had disappeared that morning –

He'd taken a pair of Rita's furry earmuffs.

Look like a right twat, don't I?

Mallary swung gently on the swings –

Not looking directly at her father.

Mallary?

Like James T. Kirk approaching an alien with his phaser, Jimmy moved forward, holding out the present.

Happy birthday.

Faced with Mallary continuing to gently swing Jimmy put the present on the ground –

Your nan misses you. She said to say 'hello'.

Like trying to tempt a pet into another room.

Suppose you'll be out clubbing tonight? Painting the town red. When I was your age I was out every night, seemed like I was out every night till I was about twenty-eight. Then you miss a Friday, then another Friday and a Saturday and then, after a bit it seems like you never go out. Enjoy it while you can.

Jimmy knew this was going to be difficult but, come on, give me something.

Eighteen's not what it was though, is it? Not like it was –

Seventeen.

What?

Today's my seventeenth birthday.

But… 2nd July, 1990…

Shit.

At that Mallary stopped swinging –

She dug her feet into the ground –

Walked away –

Stopped.

Turned around –

Came back –

Picked up the present –

And left.

Can I get your phone number?

What was it like, seeing Mallary?

We had a brilliant chat but we didn't meet for long. She had to go.

Did she ask about me?

She couldn't stop talking about you, Mum, and said she misses her grandmother very much.

That's nice, love. Thank you.

Kitty and Stevo sat in silence –

Together –

For forty-two minutes.

Fooooorrrrtyyyy-ttttwwwoooooo minutes.

With not a word.

They were watching a particularly boring –

Yet fascinating –

Bout of safety play between Mark Williams and Marco Fu.

Kitty thought:

Forty-two minutes and counting.

Without a word.

And –

And this is the shocking bit –

It didn't feel uncomfortable.

Eventually Fu went in off and Stevo broke the silence:

Why'd you like snooker, Kitty?

It scares me.

Really?

You can spend ages building a score and then, suddenly, one mistake and you've lost the frame. And it's the best-dressed sport of all.

Shall I make us a little brew, Kitty?

Christ on a bike –

Thought Kitty –

Am I falling for Stevo?

Mallary was sitting on one end of a see-saw –

With no one on the other end.

The previous night bits of Jimmy had disappeared, only his upper arms, shoulders, top of his chest, feet and head –

Minus his ears –

Remained.

The rest was invisible.

What you doing in college?

Taking an A level.

An A level? Just the one?

Janet, Mallary's mum, always said her gran and her dad were odd, best stay away from them, but, to Mallary, he looked like a right fucking nutter. Twenty-five degrees and he's dressed for the North Pole.

It seems these days kids, young adults, take three or four. One is good. A start.

Mallary looked as though she might see-saw even without anyone on the other end.

Did you enjoy it?

What?

The present. What did you do with them?

Ate some, gave some away, still got some – if Simon, the greedy pig'll stop eating them.

Simon?

Mum's latest.

Right. What's your A level in?

Science.

What type?

What you mean?

What type of science?

Science.

Suddenly Jimmy pressed down on the other end of the see-saw, lifting Mallary into the air and dumping her back down on the ground again.

Fucking hell!

Sorry. You're heavier than I thought.

Thanks a fucking bunch.

Mallary hoped whatever her dad had wasn't genetic.

The other day, what were you doing with your phone? Shaking it – like mixing a cocktail and then, yeah, cocktail phone!

If I shake it it rings.

Is that some kind of app?

No, I say to myself, if I shake my phone it'll ring.

I blow on the remote control when I watch telly and then when I change channel there'll be a woman with no clothes on.

Does it work?

This is going much better. Very nearly a conversation. Push on:

You like this park? You're here a lot?

Sit here, wait for the light to go off, in the flat. I wait for about forty minutes after the light goes off and then I go home. It's quiet there then.

Can I get on?

Jimmy took the shrug as positive so got on the see-saw.

His weight tipped Mallary up.

And there she stayed.

What you do? Work?

I got sacked. And sacked again.

Why a hundred and seventy-one?

What?

Why'd you give me a hundred and seventy-one doughnuts?

One for every one of your birthdays, for your years. One plus two plus three –

Up to eighteen.

Sorry about that. Just thought I could put all your birthdays in one box.

Let me down now.

Jimmy carefully got off his end and gently lowered his daughter to the ground.

What would you like to be when you leave college?

Qualifications don't get you nowhere these days – only deeper in debt. It's money that matters.

Out of the mouths of babes.

Did you just call your own daughter a 'babe'?

Thank you, Mallary.

For what?

I got to go. I'll see you –

Why'd you give me an Irish boy's name?

That was your mum. I wanted to call you Jill. After Jill Dando.

Didn't she get stabbed?

I wasn't to know that at the time.

It was Mallary who walked off.

Turned.

Walked back and said:

Thanks for the doughnuts.

Stevo had been plucking up the courage.

And now was the time to pluck or be plucked.

You know, Kitty, I only moved into this house cos it was left to me by my uncle. Never wanted to live in Newport. It's a funny town, isn't it?

Is this leading somewhere?

Never felt I belonged here. Until I met you.

Right. This is where it's going.

Stevo opened the cabinet of dolls and brought out a saucer that seemed to radiate.

Is that new?

Had it made yesterday.

Is there a cup to go with it?

No, just a saucer.

Stevo held it up to the light.

In the porcelain was a –

Is that?

Yes?

That's meant to be – ?

Thought you might like it. A present.

It's wonderful.

In the saucer Kitty saw an image of Kitty.

If you hold the saucer to the light you can see the picture better.

It's like a photograph. I look –

What?

You can see right through me. Why?

What?

It's not my birthday or nothing.

I just, thought it might be cool. Not cool cool, but –

Yup, it is cool. Thank you.

That's a relief, thought you might hate it.

It's the single most thoughtful thing anyone's done for me in a long time.

Shucks –

Shall I keep it in the cabinet?

Maybe not in the cabinet. Yet. Maybe, here, on the mantelpiece for now… Your hands are shaking, Kitty.

Stevo –

Like a man in a movie that's shot in light, soft focus –

And airs in the afternoon on Channel 5 –

Moves closer –

I know what you do, Kitty.

Sorry?

The phone line.

Have you been –

I've never rung it.

I'm giving that up.

I've a proposition.

Getting a part-time job.

That's good.

Better paid but I can't choose my hours –

You don't have to pay rent –

I'm not a, what do you think, that I'll sleep with you if you –

No, don't get me wrong, that's not –

I'm not –

I know –

I'm not –

It's okay –

I'm not –

I know –

I'm not –

We get on, don't we?

I'm not a prostitute.

Of course you're not, no one said you were, did they?

The tears welled up in Kitty's eyes.

By all means get this part-time job so you're still earning but if you don't have to pay rent that means you can save for that course you want to go on and we could live here together, no strings attached, like we are now, you'd still have your own space but we'd be… companions.

Kitty cried and Stevo –

Didn't know if this was a good or a bad thing.

Jimmy's phone rang.

No caller ID.

Hello?

Hello.

Kitty! I was going to call you tomorrow. Usual time, usual… well, everything. Look, I know what to do – Mallary gave me the idea, I know why I'm disappearing and I've got a plan but –

I look fantastic in porcelain.

Had she been drinking?

If you could choose to do anything, Jimmy –

She did sound a bit, well, off.

What would you do?

Jimmy wasn't sure what was going on and if that's the case you're better off saying fuck-all.

You'd like to go to Alton Towers.

Right. She is definitely pissed.

Jimmy was right about this.

Kitty had started on a bottle of Pinot and moved on to the vodka that had been in her freezer since 2013.

You are, for a fully grown man with a wonderful haircut, oddly attracted to EuroDisney. You fancy a cycling holiday. Lots of holidays. City breaks and maybe the Deep South. Come on, Jimmy, what do I want?

This wasn't the type of game he was used to playing with Kitty on the phone but –

It wasn't costing him one pound twenty pee a minute –

You want to go to a Country and Western night.

Definitely.

Gracelands.

You want to grow some veg.

You've a fondness for runner beans and some peas.

You intend to read more.

You think about poetry.

We read poetry to each other.

You eat more chips.

And kebabs.

You decide to take more baths.

Every now and again we say, 'Hang it, let's just get away for the night.' Stay in a hotel.

You bring home the small bottles of toiletries.

It's a reminder of where we stayed.

We go to the Crucible –

And fall asleep on the front row.

You convince me sponsoring a well for a village is a good thing.

Sponsor a dolphin.

Go and see dance.

Dance? You wear a cravat.

You fucking hate it.

You throw out all the clothes you haven't worn in the past year.

And then regret it.

You put in a wood burner.

And then hate it.

I start to use emojis in my texts.

I hate that.

You do the Couch to 5K.

You learn a bit more about cheese. You've often wondered what does Caerphilly actually taste like?

We do the Joe Wicks thing – prep like a boss!

I don't know who that is.

We find out what all the trees are called.

We see them every day and do we know what they are?

Same with the birds. Can you tell a sparrow from a chaffinch? Course you fucking can't.

We make love more.

All over the house.

In every room.

On the stairs.

In every wonderful position.

Sometimes fast.

Sometimes slow. You shave your pubic hair.

Into the shape of a love heart.

Or a lightning bolt.

You lose some weight. Around here.

Thanks to the Couch to 5K.

And you wear fancy hats.

And we're together –

Forever.

Jimmy was invisible –

Apart from his big toes.

So knew he had to act now –

Or never.

This is how it went:

Rise from bed.

The moonlight streamed in through the Argos blinds as –

Jimmy looked at himself in the mirror.

Not that there's anything to look at.

Hidden from the world.

It's warm, no need to put on clothes.

On to the landing –

The soothing sounds of Rita snoring.

In the kitchen Jimmy ate a banana and was amazed to see it, too, disappear.

He kept the keys firmly in his right hand –

They seemed to float of their own accord.

Into town and as he walked down Church Street it was quiet.
Left past the Riverfront and up Skinner Street –

Two big toes shuffling along the pavement.

On to Bridge Street and left and right and Pump Street and –

Right and right again.

Newport Nuts closed at 10 p.m.

Jimmy let himself in via the side door.

He looked up at the security camera in the certain knowledge
that no one could see him.

If the fucking thing was working at all –

Through the serving area –

It looked so different at night –

Another key to the office.

It was typical of Peake's shoddy management that the office
was already open –

The same sort of shoddiness –

That led to no one ever asking Jimmy to hand his keys in.

Behind the desk and the promotional shit –

Nuts hats and Nuts inflatable swimming rings shaped like big,
sticky doughnuts –

Like, seriously?

Was the safe.

Group 4 came every Wednesday to collect the contents.

Jimmy learnt the combination when Peake let it slip last
Christmas – his Army training led him to always set everything
to the same combination:

You can move quicker in a crisis.

Fucking idiot.

The little wheels on the safe seemed to spin on their own.

Zero.

Zero.

Zero.

And yes. Zero. Unbelievable, yeah?

The safe door swung open and in it lay the takings.

Exactly –

Four thousand eight hundred and twenty-seven pounds.

That's a lot of doughnuts.

Jimmy didn't count it there and then.

He put it in a Newport Nuts promotional bag and left the way he came.

Bag of cash swinging in the breeze –

Much like his own nuts –

Not caring about fingerprints or CCTV or any of that shit –

Taking the reverse route back home –

Putting the bag under his pillow as he slipped under the covers.

His duvet-covered shape distinct again in the wooden slat-filtered moonlight.

Jimmy couldn't wait for 7.30 p.m. to call Kitty.

He'd hardly slept a wink.

He knew he was nearly invisible and couldn't get caught for what he'd done last night –

The blood was still pumping a little quicker around his body.

At 8.01 a.m. he dialled the number he knew off by heart –

The premium line –

Zero.

Eight.

One pound twenty a minute well spent –

Kitty –

This number is no longer in service.

Again Jimmy dialled the number he knew so well –

The same result.

This number is no longer in service.

That's what the conversation last night was about.

It wasn't a vision of the future.

It was a vision of a future.

But not theirs.

It was a goodbye.

The last, beautiful shaft of light.

No, Kitty, you can't be gone.

He rang the number again.

Listened to the voice.

Telling him the number was no longer in service.

Why the fuck you wearing a dressing gown?

Jimmy couldn't shake the image of the Invisible Man from his mind –

A menacing figure swathed in clothes, sporting dark glasses and what he thought was called a 'smoking jacket'.

That's how Jimmy looked now standing in front of his daughter – but a Newport version of it.

Think less chic-thirties Hollywood –

More nineties Blackwood.

The only sunglasses he could find were Rita's oversized gold ones –

Sort of Goldie Lookin Chain wrapped up for the winter, you know?

For the first time Mallary invited Jimmy into her space.

She nodded to the swing next to her and Jimmy got on.

What happened to your face?

An accident.

Some fucking accident.

The air between them felt different.

And it wasn't just the cool breeze being generated by the swinging.

They both felt it.

Wha's in the bag?

Money.

Whatever you do, don't give it to me, I'll just waste it.

You can have it if you want it.

No.

You can.

What you doing with it?

Oh, I don't know, Mallary. It's a bit of a mess to be honest.

Swing higher. It's fun.

And they swang –

Is that the right word – ?

Swung –

Saying nothing as the sun sank beyond the flats –

Making the Transporter Bridge look fucking awesome.

I've been speaking with your gran.

Yeah?

I'm not saying you have to do this but we wondered if you would like to come to our house, maybe once a week.

For what?

To stay.

Overnight?

It'll be boring and Ringland takes a little getting used to and Rita is a right pain in the arse.

Will you be there?

Your gran misses you.

Okay.

What?

Be nice to go somewhere different.

Rita can clear it with your mam.

She won't care.

Like Airbnb in Ringland.

Sorry?

Nothing.

Jimmy thought it might happen now.

Is this the moment when he disappears completely and the clothes he's wearing fall to the floor and his swing stops swinging and his daughter leaves the park and carries on with her life?

They swang –

Swung.

There was silence in the park –

Apart from the creak, creak of the swings.

Nearly there.

Nearly gone.

Going.

Going…

Jimmy brought out his Samsung.

He'd shared so many fond memories with this phone.

If only it could talk.

Maybe not.

Shake it.

What?

Give it a shake. See you in Ringland, yeah?

Sorry I've been a rubbish dad.

Shit happens.

She walked away. Towards town.

And was gone.

Jimmy –

Alone in the park –

Looked at his Samsung.

He shook it and shook it and shook it and –

Fucking ring!

And it rung.

Serious.

Hello, Mum.

You still looking for a house with a squirrel hedge in the front garden?

Yes! Do you know of one?

No.

Mum?

But the Major does. He lives in a nice house in Malpas and I mentioned it and he said –

Salvation.

Was.

In.

Malpas.

It took Jimmy twenty-seven minutes to run to Malpas.

He wondered if he was sick would the sick be invisible?

Jimmy caught his breath in front of the red brick semi-bordered by two giant squirrels locked in combat.

Standing on the lawn of the man –

Who liked to garden in the nude –

He wasn't going to give up yet but –

Knew there was only a limited amount of time left –

Jimmy looked into the living room.

Standing there was a short man in a tank top illuminated by the blue flicker from the telly.

Jimmy rang the doorbell.

(A fucking Mozart tune.)

He knocked on the door.

It swung open.

Go away or I'll call the police.

Jimmy barged in, brushing Stevo to one side.

Where is she?

Get out of my house. I'm calling the police.

Jimmy checked room to room, shouting out Kitty's name – but you know when a house is empty, don't you?

Where is she, Stevo?

Truth was Stevo didn't exactly know –

But he wasn't going to admit that.

By the time Stevo entered the living room Jimmy was holding the saucer with Kitty's image in it.

What the fuck is this?

Having always dreamed of fighting for a woman, Stevo considered punching Jimmy in the face but wasn't sure how big Jimmy was under all those layers.

Jimmy thought about hitting Stevo –

But punching a man in a tank top is worse than punching a man wearing glasses.

Stevo advanced, Jimmy pulled back –

And put up his arm – the saucer with Kitty's image was a barrier between them.

The saucer –

Seemed to pulse –

Taking on a glowing green-and-blue hue.

Stevo's mouth opened and became slack as the saucer –

Slipped and tumbled from Jimmy's grasp.

In slow motion it dropped towards the ground –

Before smashing on the beige berber carpet.

The woman inside shattered –

Bits of her leapt up from the tight weave –

Racing in all directions.

Free and –

Beautifully broken.

Where is she, Stevo?

Goes to show how much you know her – she's starting her new job tonight. And after she's finished she's coming home, to me.

Her new job.

If Stevo could see Jimmy's face –

He'd see the horror on it.

Me and Kitty are going to make a go of it.

All the fight went out of Jimmy.

Kitty was at her 'new job' and he was about to disappear.

He shut the garden gate in the shadow of the giant duelling squirrels and headed back the way he came.

Stevo watching him, framed in the light from the front door.

The Number 73 bus went by –

On the side of it, a picture of Mark Williams smiling and holding his snooker cue –

The bus hit a pothole and a brown pool of water soaked Jimmy.

Cheers, Mark, nice one.

Under the street lights, he passed Aldi and a seagull shat all over the back of his dressing gown.

While wiping that off he stepped in dog shit.

He knew if he took his shoes off now he'd only have one big toe left.

He was about to disappear without finding the woman he loved.

The night seemed darker than usual.

It began to rain.

Fucking bloody perfect.

Past the Queensway, Upper Dock Street, Cambrian Road.

He knew where he would go to disappear:

Newport Nuts.

Maybe he'll put the money back – really fuck with Peake's head.

He was guided to Newport Nuts by its neon sign.

The stars were out.

Barely visible through Newport's night-light pollution.

Jimmy circled his former place of employment and –

Standing next to the coin bin where the intercom had devoured so many doughnut orders stood Kitty. Jimmy dropped the bag of cash at his feet.

What you doing here?

Fancied a doughnut but…

A notice on the door said:

Closed until further notice.

The place was wrapped in black and yellow police tape.

The place would never reopen.

Due to Jimmy's actions?

No. The people of Newport decided they weren't going to put their money in a bin.

Have you been to… work?

Couldn't go through with it.

Jimmy didn't know how this might go.

For him.

And for Kitty.

I promised I'd never say it but I love you.

Jimmy?

I love you. But I really am disappearing.

I believe you.

About the love or the disappearing?

The wind picked up the cash and it began to scatter, dancing in the air.

Jimmy and Kitty watched the money float back towards the people who'd originally spent it.

The red-and-yellow neon lights advertising Newport Nuts then flickered, flickered and died.

One by one the street lights around Jimmy and Kitty went out.

The twenty-four-hour glow from the Friar's Walk shopping centre became as dark as a hedge-fund manager's heart.

Leaving only the moon and the stars as weak illumination.

Tell me.

What?

Anything. Please. Just talk to me, Kitty. I always want to hear your wonderful voice.

As Kitty spoke –

Jimmy closed his eyes and settled into the sound of her familiar tones.

There was a girl, let's call her Catherine, and when she was around fifteen years old if she could have flicked a switch and it meant she didn't exist she would have done so.

As she spoke Jimmy removed his clothes. He took off his earmuffs and hat in one swift motion.

Jimmy took off his dressing gown.

Keep talking to me, Kitty. Please.

Catherine chose to lose herself – since she was a little girl she turned away from everything. Sometimes she longed to be…

His stupid glasses and tracksuit top –

When she got a bit older she was wild – on purpose. That's how people who can't be loved act, isn't it? It's difficult to be close to people when you're feeling like you want to disappear. As an adult Catherine did a job where she doesn't meet anyone, slipping between the cracks of a town that's slipping between the cracks, she's kind to strangers she can never meet and dreams of studying for a course that analyses what people do – instead of actually doing something herself. She doesn't feel part of anything and no one understands. Until she meets someone…

As Jimmy took off his floral scarf from around his head with the two holes poked out for him to see, Kitty undid the buttons on her shirt –

Her shirt off.

His trainers.

Her shoes.

His tracksuit bottoms.

Her skirt and tights.

He took off his pants.

She took off her pants and bra.

Until there was nothing left.

A pile of clothes at his feet.

A pile of clothes at hers.

Can you see me, Kitty?

The smallest of smiles from Kitty.

Newport's very own Mona Lisa.

The not knowing was torture for Jimmy.

She reached out a hand.

Jimmy touched it, their fingers creating a bridge.

Light flowed from Kitty and into Jimmy and spilled out and filled the car park.

Is this... altruism?

Far from it.

Their light illuminating the surrounding streets.

An effervescent glow radiating outwards.

And outwards.

Until the whole town took on this glow.

With this one touch Newport, glorious Newport, turned from dark to light.

People looked out of their windows and wondered where all this light was coming from.

They poured out on to the streets to enjoy the midnight radiance.

Standing next to the coin bin were two lights shining for each other.

Jimmy and Kitty were made of light.

From head to toe to fingertip.

Burning brightly in the centre of the universe.

In the car park of a drive-through doughnut restaurant in Newport.

(*End of the play.*)

A Nick Hern Book

How My Light Is Spent first published in Great Britain in 2017 as a paperback original by Nick Hern Books Limited, The Glasshouse, 49a Goldhawk Road, London W12 8QP, in association with the Royal Exchange Theatre, Theatre by the Lake and Sherman Theatre

How My Light Is Spent copyright © 2017 Alan Harris

Alan Harris has asserted his right to be identified as the author of this work

Designed and typeset by Nick Hern Books, London
Printed in Great Britain by CPI Books (UK) Ltd

A CIP catalogue record for this book is available from the British Library

ISBN 978 1 84842 620 7